PURE HELL
—BUT—
I MADE IT

Only Women Bleed

CE PAULS

Order this book online at www.trafford.com
or email orders@trafford.com

Most Trafford titles are also available at major online book retailers.

Printed in the United States of America.

ISBN: 978-1-4669-8190-4 (sc)
ISBN: 978-1-4669-8189-8 (e)

Trafford rev. 02/20/2013

 www.trafford.com

North America & international
toll-free: 1 888 232 4444 (USA & Canada)
phone: 250 383 6864 ♦ fax: 812 355 4082

CONTENTS

Foreword

*T*HIS BOOK WAS WRITTEN in hopes of reaching those who believe that they are alone, and to ensure them that they can have hope by knowing that others that have experienced what they are going through . . . and are willing to help them.

Be strong, survive. Although it hurts, and you feel as if you can't go on, it gets easier. The pain you feel today will only be a memory tomorrow. The scars we get from this life we live make us strong for the life we have yet to live.

. . . Ce Pauls

$\mathcal{W}$HEN I BEGAN TO write this book, I had no idea it would be a book. I'm not a psychologist or hold any other title. It is my hope that by exposing my trials to others that my experiences and survival of these will help those in need.

The book begins with a trauma from my childhood. It ends with poetry and phone numbers of helpful organizations.

I hope that I have not offended anyone in my family, but I feel that writing this book was very necessary.

THE DREAM

May 13, 1973 (Age 12)

I WOKE UP IN a cold sweat. My brother had been shot. There was blood everywhere, gushing from his head. Then I realized it was just a nightmare. Vivid, and so real and in color. I shook it off.

I jumped out of bed, realizing it was Friday. I must get ready to go water-skiing. We had a lease to a private lake that we went to every weekend. We water-skied, fished, ice skated in winter and hunted. Flushed with excitement, I dressed and ran upstairs where my parents were fixing breakfast.

They asked me if I was ready for a day on the lake. I told them that I was. Father assured me that we would be on our way as soon as I ate.

I was first to put my things in the truck. Weekends were my very favorite times of the week, and water-skiing was by far my most favorite recreation. I had just begun to water-ski in slalom tournaments, and

I loved everything about the sport. I grew up at that lake. It was the happiest time in my life. By the time I was 5 years old I could water ski and by the age of 8 I was skiing on one ski.

Mother and father were in the middle of a fight with my sister, Ann, who was two years older than I was. She had little interest in water sports and it was always a chore to get her to go to the lake, away from her friends.

I went to the truck to wait for my parents and listen to the radio. Elton John sang "Daniel." For some odd reason, the words touched my heart. Overhead, an airplane caught my attention, in particular its flashing red beacon. I remember thinking to myself how strange it was for the plane to have its beacon light on in the day. I was 13 years old and didn't know that all planes have lights on them. I stared at the plane as the words to "Daniel" touched my heart. My first thought was of my brother Wayne. The song made me think of Wayne in sadness. Which was odd since when ever I thought about my brother it was always with a smile. He could make everyone laugh. He was kind and was always there to lend a helping hand. However, he did have a temper when things didn't quit go his way. He was always busy, and had enough energy for 3 people. I loved him dearly and missed him since he was in the Navy and stationed in San Diego.

Then, something earthbound caught my eye. A white car pulled up in front of the house. Two men in beige uniforms got out. I remember thinking how ugly the uniforms were. As they walked past the truck they tossed a fleeting glance at me with empty eyes, and without a word approached the front door. Mother and Father were in the doorway of the house when the uniformed men motioned for them to go back into the house and accompanied them in.

Dismissing our strange visitors, I continued to sit in the truck while the strains of "Daniel" filled the cabin. I had heard the song many times before, but today there was something about it that was different. The words were melancholy, almost painful in their presentation. I turned off the radio and went inside the house, not prepared for what I was about to witness.

Mother was crying uncontrollably. Ann screamed hysterically. Father stared at the floor in disbelief. Suddenly, my thoughts went back to my nightmare the night before. I realized that my nightmare was a premonition, my brother Wayne was dead. No one spoke. Words weren't necessary; I just knew he was dead.

As a sailor in the U.S. Navy, Wayne's special place was Spain. In the song ("Daniel," Spain is mentioned, headed for Spain. Wayne had lived a short, but somewhat tormented life, and now he was at peace with the almighty, having fallen victim to a bullet. His mortal scars were healed. ("Do you still feel the pain of the scars that won't heal?") more words from the song touched me so deeply.

Death is one of the hardest things to go through. For parents it becomes almost unbearable. When there are other kids in the family at times they are left to mourn by themselves. My parents had no idea how much pain I was in, I cried in silence and I wasn't going to add my grief to theirs.

THE FUNERAL

*E*VERYONE DRESSED IN BLACK, their faces gray, solemn and expressionless. I sat in a corner, facing a television set as lifeless as my brother, Wayne. Surely someone would explain to me what this all meant. Finally Father indicated it was time for us to go. The past two days had been so very hard on all of us, especially mother. I hoped the turmoil would end soon. I wasn't sure what my parents were talking about, but I was about to find out. The family walked outside. There was a black limousine in the driveway. As we piled into the car my parents were worried about one of my sisters. Fae, was pregnant with her first baby. The family was very concern about how Waynes' death might affect her physically.

The engine of the big black car droned as it carried us down the street. All I knew was that it had something to do with Wayne. I remember thinking, he's dead, so why don't they just leave us be. And why do they all cry, and say that it's better this way? At 13 years old I didn't understand how someone being dead was for the better. He was young and healthy. He was finally enjoying life in the Navy. My head hurt from all of the noise I was hearing. Death, Better to be dead at such a young age of 17 years old, a life lost, how? why? When will this all stop?

The car stopped and we all got out. An old, spooky man, garbed in a black tux, led us to a darkened room. A wall separated us from people on the other side. I couldn't see them, but in my mind's eye I knew they were there. At the front of the room, ahead of all the chairs, there was a beautiful silver box. It took me a while, but I knew that my brother—or at least his body—was lying in that box. I remember thinking, how will I ever be sure. I was compelled to rush forward and look inside, however, that wasn't allowed. I never found out. The box was never opened.

During what they called the eulogy, Fae began screaming and sobbing incessantly. She said she couldn't believe that Wayne was dead. Mother and my other brother, Shelby, did their best to calm her. It wasn't enough; Fae sobbed for quite a long time. Everyone was so afraid that she was going to go into labor, or worse lose her baby.

Through all this a somber man talked about my brother and expressed how Wayne had positively influenced our lives. How did he know? I had never seen him before. He didn't know by brother, he had never met my brother. I found myself angry at this. Why doesn't anyone who really knew Wayne talk about him? As his narrative concluded, I heard rustling on the other side of the wall. Then silence. The man in the black tux gestured to us and pointed to the silver box. I thought to myself, maybe I'll be able to see inside. Again, I was disappointed. The family approached the closed box and stared at it. No one spoke, we just stood there. It was unbearable. I thought the moment would never end. I was so confused as to what we were doing. Why can't I look in the silver box? Where is my brother, I need to see him to believe he is dead.

As we walked to the door leading to the long, black car, I turned and looked at the silver box one last time. The room had fallen silent, and empty, except for the vacant chairs and the silver box that I knew wasn't empty. A feeling of deep sadness cut into my core, and loneliness enveloped me. The song "Daniel" played over and over in my head (your eyes have died, but you see more than I).

I didn't want to get into the limousine . . . I couldn't . . . I needed to see what, or who, was in the silver box. I began to scream. Father and Shelby forced me into the car, as I screamed and tore at them. Before long, the long, black car lumbered out onto the street. I hoped we were going home, but I sensed that wasn't our direction. Rain pelted the car as the gunmetal gray (surely the color of the gun that took Waynes' life) skies opened. I asked Shelby where we were going. He remarked, "To the cemetery."

Upon entering the graveyard I could see nothing but cold headstones, they all were the same, dead stones. Ahead of the car, I saw a white canopy in the distance. Beneath it, the silver box. My mind raced, faster and faster. How can it be here? I left it behind in that darkened room.

The family sat in the first row, near the silver box. A group of men in military attire stood motionless in the rain. Seven men in uniform with rifles. They were beautiful. Another man in uniform raised a bugle to his lips and played the most haunting melody I have ever heard. They called it Taps. Then, without expression, the seven men pointed their rifles to the sky and began to shoot. Startled, and very scared, I remembered hearing that sound before. In my nightmare. Three shots, the 21-gun salute. To this day that haunting song and the gun fire tear through my heart.

The silver box was draped with the American flag. Uniformed men standing around the box gently lifted the flag and began folding it. When they were finished one of the men walked to my mother and handed her the triangularly shaped cloth.

Finally, we got back into the car. Shelby comforted me and told me that we were going home now. I was glad it was over. I wondered if the silver box was going to be at the house waiting for us, just as it had followed us to the cemetery. I refused to believe that my brother was in the silver box, and no one could tell me differently.

As the years passed, this part of my life followed me and haunted me. My nightmare revisited me from time to time. Under its power I could see Wayne walking down the street. Sometimes, he would enter my bedroom and tell me that I was strong and that I would endure the much heartache to come. He was right.

May 18, 1973

I wanted to go back to school. There was only two weeks left and I missed my friends. My mother told me that it was okay but she wanted to take me. I told her that I needed to walk.

My best friend at the time came up to me and asked me where I had been. I told her that my brother had just died. She told me I was lying and that it wasn't a funny joke. I could hardly deal with what she had said; the school sent me home. She did call that night and apologize for being insensitive. It was hard to believe. I was angry, not at her but at my brother for dying. People at times don't know what to say in this kind of situation. You get mad at them for not saying anything, yet they don't always say the right thing. Don't blame them. It's not their fault. Let it go forgive them for what ever they may say out of loss for words.

May 20, 1973

My mother and father went to bed early that night. I waited for about ten to fifteen minutes to be sure they wouldn't come out of their room. Then, I found an empty Pepsi liter bottle. I rinsed it out and opened the liquor cupboard that I wasn't supposed to be in, grabbed the bourbon and poured a hefty portion into the Pepsi bottle. Then, I replaced the bourbon I took with water. They would never know. I took the Pepsi bottle down to my room and carefully put it between the wall and my bed so that it couldn't be seen, even if someone looked under the bed. This was the start of me trying to exterminate the feelings of loneliness.

One week later it was still hard to get out of bed, even to go to school. Thank goodness, I had only a few more days until summer vacation.

It had become a ritual every morning. I would wake up, and, before getting out of bed, take out the Pepsi bottle and gulp two big swigs of bourbon. It didn't taste bad anymore. I'd become numb to the flavor. It didn't even give me a headache.

After bracing myself with alcohol, I'd get ready for school and be almost oblivious to what was going on around me by the time I reached school.

Staggering into class, I asked Ron, my boyfriend at the time, if he wanted to go to my house for lunch. He agreed, so at lunchtime he and three of my other friends strolled to my house.

When we arrived, I realized that I had left my house key in my school locker. I was furious. Ron and the rest suggested that we go back and eat in the lunchroom. That idea made me angrier. I checked all of the windows and doors. All locked. I went to the back of the house and by that time my classmates were begging me to go back to school.

I looked around the yard and saw some railroad ties. They were about four feet long. I picked one up and threw it through a basement window as my friends stared at me in disbelief. Ron crawled through the broken window and opened the back door.

Once inside, I headed to the cupboard. It took two large swigs to calm me down. I passed the bottle to my friends and we laughed about the window. Dad would never know. I was his baby and there was no way he would suspect me. He always blamed my sister Ann, who was failing school and spent most of her time in trouble. After all, I was a straight A student, and never in trouble.

Most alcoholics have a hard time maintaining a former lifestyle, but my grades never dropped. Unusual indeed, when you consider that I drank most of the time leading to my eighteenth birthday.

May 26, 1973 (Age 15)

My lunch time adventure was so well received one of my friends asked if I'd like to join the gang at his house for lunch. I asked if there would be alcohol and he assured me that drinks were on the menu. That made me even more anxious to go with him.

His parents only had beer, but it was enough to get us buzzed. We arrived back at school early, so we went to the gym where a volleyball game was in progress. I loved to play volleyball and was soon in the midst of the action. How was I supposed to know it was a tournament match? It didn't take long for the coach took me aside and politely asked me to leave. He wasn't sure if I had been drinking but I know he suspected as much. He instructed my group to meet with him after school. As it turned out, only one of us appeared. The sober one, not me.

The next morning, the coach came into our class. "Those of you who where in the gym yesterday and weren't supposed to be, I want to see you in the principal's office now." We were scared.

Fortunately, the principal and the coach realized it was our first incident and as we were straight A students, they let us off with a firm warning. I left the principal's office feeling pretty good. If I were lucky, my parents would never hear of the incident.

As I was leaving, the coach called to me. I responded and he asked if we could talk. He put his arm around my shoulder. He told me that he was well aware that this wasn't the first time I came to school drunk. He encouraged me to get help. Of course, I denied the whole thing and told him I didn't know what he was talking about. Inside, though, I kept asking myself how much does he know? It must have been the smell of the alcohol on my breath. I'd to be more careful in the future. The coach also told me that he would not be back the next year and that he wanted me to keep in touch, particularly if there was anything he could do help me. However the next year I would be in a new school as well. Middle school.

The words he said that day were strong. He told me how I would be ruining my life if I kept on drinking, and it simply wouldn't be worth it. I don't believe he knew how much alcohol had already crept into my life. I had already attempted suicide, without success, managing only to make myself dreadfully sick. I couldn't stop drinking, either; it was so easy to wash away the pain with two or three swigs of bourbon.

Sometimes parents overlook the obvious. Before my brother's death my parents never worried about me. Out of six children, I singularly received A's on my report card. I loved school and was usually upset if illness forced me to miss a day. My parents were never confronted with attending a teacher conference; there was never a need. I seldom, if ever, complained. And I never made unreasonable demands. I only asked for the things that I needed. I talked only when spoken to and was considerate of my parent's friends. In other words, I thought of myself as a model child.

After Wayne died, I was constantly in need of affection. Hugs and kisses and kind words were at the top of my list. But that soon disappeared. There was a point where I couldn't stand to be touched. I felt that I was unworthy of affection, how could I be worthy being drunk all the time? I hated myself more and more. Concurrently, I searched for answers to the mysteries of death, and I would talk about death to almost everyone. Why does it happen? Where do people go when they die?

I didn't realize it then, but my parents were so much into their own pain that they didn't notice what was happening to me. On the surface, nothing had changed; I was still their little angel. My report cards were garnished with A's and I continued to be their same sweet daughter. All the while, I was in pursuit of my next drink.

While in school, I shared many of my poems with my friends. They laughed and said to me that only a crazy person would write such depressing things down on paper. However, by doing so, I was able to express myself and not hold these things in my heart. I believe that had I not written them down, I would be a very bitter woman today. I had no one to talk to about my pain therefore I had to do something with it.

Middle school was a good time for me. I got into gymnastics and did quit well. I didn't drink as much then. My best friend of elementary school started to hang out with other friends but we still remained friends. Then off to high school.

★   ★   ★

Sitting on the front lawn of the high school, I had decided against going to my next class. The bell rang and everyone else went inside. I was sitting there alone and I heard a voice call my name. I looked up. It was one of my friend's friends. I didn't like him very much. He never treated her very well.

He called me over to the car. I thought he might have a message for his girlfriend. I got up and went over to the car. He asked my name and asked if I was her friend. I said that I was. He then grabbed my arm. I pulled but couldn't get free. He began pushing me into his car. I screamed. No one was around to hear me. I kept screaming and his hold on me got tighter and painful. He jumped in the car after me and I tried to get out the other side. He pulled me back in the car and sped off. He pulled out of the parking lot and began to go faster. He was still holding my arm and I was struggling. I made him swerve and he got mad and hit me. I was stunned. We were traveling about 60 mph. I thought to myself, could I jump? No, I would be dead the minute I hit the ground. Not a bad thing, but I was scared and at that point I wanted to live. I asked him where he was taking me. He said just to talk. I knew that was a lie. If he just wanted to talk why was he forcing me into his car.

He was from a very rich family and his father was well known. He had a nice car and nice clothes. It just didn't figure in my mind what was going to happen to me.

He pulled up to a house not far from school. A very large house with a manicured lawn. There were many cars out front; I hoped that someone was home. He dragged me out of the car and into the house. The house was evidently vacant of anyone. He told me that no one would ever hear me scream. He was right. I tried to run for the door when he let go of me. He hit me across the face and grabbed my arm. He then dragged me to the stairs and pulled me down them.

In a bedroom in the basement, he tied my hands to the bedpost with his belt. He then got undressed and pulled my pants off. Screaming and kicking did nothing to stop him. I had never been with a boy before and the pain was unbearable. He was brutal with me and I hated him. I pleaded with him. Told him if he let me go I wouldn't tell anyone. He just laughed. He said no one would believe me anyway. Given his families reputation he could get away with anything. When he was finished with me he dragged me to the car again and drove me back to school. He warned me never to say a word to anyone or he would kill me. He said he could even get away with murder if he wanted to. I believed him.

School was letting out and I waited until all of the buses were gone. One of my girlfriends saw me along side of the building. She yelled for the driver to stop, but they wouldn't. I walked home in pain and ashamed. I felt dirty and worthless. When I got home I took a long shower. I couldn't get his smell off of me. The harder I scrubbed the worse it got. I then turned to an old friend, bourbon. It deadened the pain and my mind.

I never told anyone about that day. I believed him. I avoided any conversations with him. I avoided his girlfriend and all of his classes. If it even meant staying out of my classes to avoid him I did. I would go to class later to get the assignments.

I told myself that I just had to forget what had happened and move on. The alcohol seemed to help me forget.

No one should have to go through that type of pain. Because of those people who have sick minds, there is a chance it will happen. My life was never the same after that day. The remembrance of that is still with me today. If you have ever been through this, there is help for you. It is not right for someone to violate you in this way. Counseling is available for people to cope with the feelings they have after going through this. The person that violates another should go to jail. So he (or she) will never be able to do this to anyone else. If we stand by and say nothing as I did, he may do it again to someone else. Maybe your attacker is related to you. Get help, get counseling and put these people in jail.

A year later, we moved to a little town east of Denver. It was a very small town and I was given more freedom than I'd ever had. My sisters, Mary, Ann and Fae, were now on their own, as was my remaining brother, Shelby. They had all begun to have families of their own. I didn't want to have kids. The agony I had endured to this point, and seeing my parents go through such pain, was much more than I thought possible.

The school was great. Small classes and nice teachers. I began to date the man who brought the mail to our little town. He was nice and never wanted much from me. He had been married once before. We dated about six months and then he, too, left me. He went back to his ex-wife. Not many tears were shed. I wasn't ready to be serious with anyone. By this time I was only drinking with friends for fun. The town seemed to do me good. I had more freedom then I had ever had.

Months later, I began dating a man who was a herdsman for a cattle company. I was seventeen and began drinking more. He took me to fancy restaurants and we would spend a lot of time at his house. My mother and father liked him a lot and trusted him with me. He told me he loved me and would like to get married someday. He decided it would be best not to tell anyone until I was eighteen. I agreed. We would take long walks in the woods and would make love under the stars. He was so very special.

One day I knew there was something wrong. I talked to my counselor about it. He told me that I might be pregnant. The counselor agreed to take me to the next town to have a test done. He almost lost his job over it. After the test was over the doctor came out and announced that I was in fact pregnant. The counselor told me I would have to tell my parents.

When we got back to the school, the principal was waiting for us. He had already told my mother and father. He told the counselor to go home and think about what kind of jeopardy he put his job in and that he would talk to him later. The principal took me down to the store that my parents owned. My mother was waiting outside. She hugged me and said that everything was going to be fine, and then sent me home. When my parents got home, we talked. My father was very calm and understanding. I told him I would have to go to my boyfriend's and that we would make a decision on what we were going to do. I took my mother's car and drove to his house. He wasn't there, so I drove to the barn where he groomed the cattle. He was attending a steer and listening to Bobby Vinton recordings.

I told him that we needed to talk. He took me to his office and I told him that we were about to become parents. He looked at me in disbelief. He then got mad and told me that he wasn't about to marry me or have a screaming brat to take care of. I was very calm. In a way I knew that was going to be his answer. I walked out without saying a word and got into the car. Now the decision was mine. I didn't want to live.

I loved him and wanted to have his baby. But I was seventeen, too young to do it on my own. I couldn't bear to watch my parents go through any more pain. As I was driving I decided that I would just run the car off of the cliff and die. I waited for the steepest cliff. I pulled hard on the steering wheel. Nothing. The car wasn't turning. I let go of the wheel thinking it would hit the wall on the other side of the road. The car remained on the road. I wasn't driving anymore. Someone else was.

Surely it wasn't God's will for me to die just yet. I grabbed the wheel again and drove home. When I got home I told my parents that I had decided to have an abortion. That he wasn't interested in having me by his side, let alone a kid. My father hugged me and told me he was proud of me.

It's hard to keep things from others in a small town. I stayed out of school for the next two weeks. My mother took me to a larger town nearby and I had an abortion. It was the hardest thing I've ever done. The abortion took only ten minutes—the longest ten minutes of my life. Only ten minutes to kill a child. I felt like I wanted to die. But I survived. At age seventeen it's hard to make such a big decision, but I had to. It was my body and my life.

People dispute the fact that abortion kills, and it does. However, the point I want to make is that at seventeen I was but a child myself. There was no way that I would be able to take care of a baby, financially or emotionally. I needed to grow up.

To bring a child into this world without a father—and without the right state of mind—would be cruel. Children need a mother and a father along with so many needs. I would realize later in life that one parent can do just fine. However, I could not have given this child anything at that point in my life. Abortion is not the only option. Before you do what I did get all of the facts. Pray about it, God will give you the answer.

No one knows what goes through a girl's mind when she's experienced something like this in her life—the guilt of killing a living being. Feeling dirty, and certain that she doesn't deserve to live. No one should have to face this alone. There are many helpful organizations that are there for you. If you find yourself in this situation alone, be strong and don't let it overcome you. You aren't dirty, and, yes, you are a good person. Everyone makes mistakes. Just learn from them. You'll never be the same person you once were. Each time God puts you through a challenge, you grow. To grow in God and to ask for his help is a wonderful thing.

No one has a definitive answer for how to deal with something like this. They may have been through the same thing, but everyone's different and individuals cope with things differently. Follow your heart and pray for an answer from God. He's the one who can and will guide you.

Abortion may not be the right thing for you. That's why you need to talk to someone about it. Don't keep these feelings of despair locked inside. If you've no one to talk to, or even if you have someone to talk to, write your feelings down. Keep a journal. By doing so you'll release an enormous amount of pain onto the page.

Feelings of despair overtook me at times. I would cut myself with anything I could find. I felt as if I would be alone forever. Then, Bill, a boy in my class began to pay attention to me. He was nice and always told me that I was beautiful. Before that year Bill wasn't interested in me and I had not really noticed him much either.

We spent a lot of time together, maybe two or three months. One night, while we were watching TV at my house, my dog signaled to go out. I went to the back door and didn't notice that Bill was behind me. As I opened the door for the dog, Bill's sudden appearance startled me. With my hand on the door jam, he slammed the door. The metal bit into my hand on the door. I tried not to scream and alarm my parents. Bill said he didn't see my hand. For some reason, I didn't believe him.

After that incident, Bill changed. He would tell me what to wear, and how to wear my hair. He frequently called me "Stupid." "How could anyone love you?" he would ask. Two months into our friendship, I began to believe him.

When someone constantly tells you how stupid you are, that you are ugly and no one would ever love you except them, you start to believe them.

One night following a basketball game, we returned to my house. Our school lost the game, and he felt he was to blame. He took his anger out on me. He told me it was my fault that he didn't do well. That if I had been more supportive before the game, he would have done better. Then he cried and told me that he loved me. He said that he wanted to marry me and revealed his plan for our elopement. He showered me with compliments and told me that he would die if I ever left him. That he wanted us to be together forever. I felt loved so I said yes.

We would drive to a nearby city and find someone of authority to marry us. We left a note for my parents. In it we asked my family not to worry, that we loved each other and we would call them from our destination. Bill's foster parents lived in the house next to my parents, so we asked mother and father to relay our actions to them.

As we neared the city, we realized that in the state of Colorado minors must have the consent of their parents to marry. Turning north, we headed to Cheyenne, Wyoming, thinking that we could be married there without a parent's approval. It was Sunday, and in Cheyenne, everything was closed.

I phoned my parents and they urged us to return home, saying that if we still wanted to get married after a "cooling off period", they would arrange a ceremony for us. That did it! We headed back to Colorado.

After talking the matter over with my parent and his foster parents, we visited his adoptive parents. While we had received the blessings from my parents and his foster parents, Bill's adoptive parents were sure that I was taking their son away from the Lord. His mother said that I would burn in hell. Then she asked if I was pregnant. I told her that we'd never had sex so that was impossible. She then told me that time would tell. She didn't believe me.

We set our date to be married on Christmas, the day after my 18th birthday, and the beginning of my adulthood. Mother made me a dress and Bill bought me a ring. The wedding was small, but nice. After the wedding we headed for the city, again, but this time we were on our honeymoon.

Our room at the Motel 6 was on the second floor, up a flight of steep stairs. Bill led the way, a suitcase in one hand and a bottle of champagne in the other. I juggled two bottles of champagne and lifted my dress to climb the stairs. That's when I heard a man's voice coming from one of the rooms below. First a wolf call, and then a whistle. Bill was furious. He turned and I thought he was going back downstairs to confront the man, but instead he took the bottle of champagne and hit me across the head. Glass shattered and I felt the warmth of blood dripping down my face. Dizzily, I came close to falling, but managed to regain my balance. The bottles I was carrying toppled to the floor and shattered.

Bill helped me up the stairs to our room where he cleaned out the cut on my head and softly said he was sorry. In his remorse, he explained how I was his now and he just couldn't stand for anyone else to look at me. I hated him at that point, but felt trapped beyond belief.

If I had only realized Bill was inclined to suffer fits of insane jealously. I didn't know what to do. I couldn't bear to look at him.

Men like Bill never change. Don't ever think that you can change a man with your love. A person has to want to change. Remember that you can only change yourself, if you want to.

It took three days for my wound to heal. That meant three days closer to Bill than I wanted to be. Finally, I was able to cover up most of the bruise with makeup. Thanks to my groom, the headache stayed with me for three days after our departure. It didn't take a doctor to convince me I had a concussion. My fear of serious injury told me I should report the incident to someone, but I was equally afraid of the prospect of someone blaming me, at least in part, for the occurrence. After all, Bill and I were married and I felt that I needed to work on my marriage like my parents did.

At first we lived in a small apartment in a very small town. When Bill left for work he would lock the door behind him. I had no key, so in effect I was locked in all day. He said he didn't trust me. Sometimes, I would unlatch the window and crawl out just to get some fresh air.

One day he came home beaten up for what seemed to be no reason. I kept asking him what I had done wrong. He gave no answer. Then he told me the culprit was a man that he used to run drugs for. According to Bill, the man beat him up after learning that Nathan was out of the drug business. And that wasn't all. His assailant advised him that he would forgive Bill's indebtedness to him, if he would ". . . get his lovely wife to hook for him for about two months." I didn't understand what that meant. Bill explained that I was to sell my body. That put me in the middle of things.

When Bill suggested that I go along with the payoff arrangement, I resoundingly said no. Moreover, I told him to go to Hell. That's when he struck me. When the old man who lived above us responded to my screams, Bill told him that I had fallen in the tub and that I was okay. Not convinced, the man asked to speak to me. I yelled through the door that I was fine. It was the coward's way out, but I was so scared of being beaten that I did what I was told. Besides that I was afraid of what my husband would do to the frail old man.

The thing that I didn't realize was that men like Nathan never get better without professional help. In fact, they may get worse. The beatings may occur more frequent with greater severity. Your attacker will often prey on your self-esteem and make you feel that you deserve the punishment you are receiving. Nothing could be further from the truth. If you should need help, ask for it. It's not worth risking your life for self-pride. If people believe that you are stupid for getting into a situation like this, let them think it. In truth, it's not your fault.

One of the pre-marriage agreements that Bill presented me with, was that I throw away all of my Starsky and Hutch pictures, and that I never watch the TV show again. At first I thought that was dumb, but eventually I consented to do so. I didn't need to be surrounded by all of my childish habits.

But out of sight wasn't necessarily out of mind. While sitting at home alone in the middle of the afternoon, I decided to watch Starsky and Hutch. It seemed innocent enough to indulge in one of life's little pleasures. Besides, Bill wouldn't be home for hours. Surely one TV show would do no harm.

But fate wasn't in my favor that day. For some reason Bill came home early. I was in the kitchen preparing lunch when I heard the front door slam. As I entered the living room Bill attacked me. He slapped me so hard that I fell to the ground. He then turned his attention to the TV, kicking in its screen. Sparks went everywhere. Resuming his attack on me, he kicked me in the ribs. Grabbing my arm, he pulled me close to his face. He was screaming at me, telling me that I had disobeyed him and that this was my punishment.

He turned, walked out of the house, got into his car and drove off. At that point I should have called my parents to come and get me. But I didn't, the only thing I did was start to make him the best dinner I had ever made. A peace offering, if you will.

We stayed with my parents for one month, and then with his for two months. Both of us understood that we needed a place of our own. While we were with his parents, I was introduced to God. I was excited about learning about the Lord. Bill, on the other hand, was not. He disliked the church almost as much as he hated his adoptive parents, and he wanted out.

That's when we found a house to rent in a small town hardly more than an hour from my parent's house. The house was in between two stockyards so the smell was unbearable at times, but not as unbearable as the suffering at the hands of my husband.

In retrospect, Bill quit High School five months before graduation. I lacked only had one credit of English to complete, so I made up the shortfall by creating my own newspaper. I filled the pages with stories of battered women and sad poems. Of course, the school believed that my "news stories" were imaginary. They had no idea the stories were true, and I was the one being beaten.

As graduation drew near, I talked about college and how I was going to become a great artist. My portfolio was polished, and I was adding to it daily.

One night, Bill, in one of his fits of rage, told me that I would never amount to anything. He said he planned to keep me confined, that if I thought that I was going to college, and be around other men, I was mistaken. He then went to the other room and brought out my portfolio. He told me that all of the pictures were trash and should be burned. He dumped my collection in the middle of the living room and doused them with lighter fluid. A moment later my dreams were ablaze.

I screamed and begged him not to destroy my works. He told me that my God couldn't help. He said that I was placed on this earth to serve him and no one else. I ran to the kitchen to get water to put out the fire. By the time the flames were extinguished all was ruined. My contempt for Bill exceeded all boundaries. I couldn't recreate my portfolio. My dream was shattered. Afterwards, every time I would try to draw, even in my rare times of peace, all I could see were flames. I put my paints and brushes in the trash . . . with all my hopes. Fifteen years would pass before I would clasp another brush. Or create any art work.

As you can see, Bill was demented. He would tell me that I was ugly and that it was unlikely that anyone else would ever want me. But in case they did, he assured me that he would beat my face in an attempt to change their mind.

He would tell me that I was good for nothing, including homemaking. One night he came home to the sight of two boys playing in the road in front of our house. One of them was about eight years old, the other barely twelve. Storming into the house, Bill angrily accused me of having sex with the older boy. I didn't even know that the boys were playing near our house. Again I was slapped around until I couldn't see. That night he raped me repeatedly. I was bruised from head to toe.

The day after, I went to an Avon party with one of my sisters. When I got home Bill was sitting in his chair. Usually, my dog would greet me at the door. Not this day. I noticed that Bill had his pellet gun out. I asked him where my dog was and he said she had tried to bite him so he kicked her and she was under the bed. I rushed to the bedroom, not knowing whether to expect to see my dog alive or dead. She was, scared, but breathing.

The next day, after Bill had left for work, the dog came out. I gave her a haircut and was alarmed to find that her back contained fourteen pellets and eight Bb's. I bathed her and dressed her wounds. She would be okay. However, my hate for him grew.

When Bill got home I confronted him about her. He flew into a rage and said that it must have been those boys who were playing in the road. He ran out of the house "to go kill them," as he put it. I pulled him back. I didn't want him to hurt them. I guess deep down that I knew who really hurt my dog.

As graduation neared, I was very excited. I waited for the announcement in the mail. I wasn't sending announcements, but the school said they would let me know where and when to be there. When the announcement was long overdue, I asked Bill if he had seen it in the mail. He said he had, but thrown it away. I asked him if he remembered the date and time of the event. He told me that I needed to be at the school at 7:30 the evening of June 23, 1979.

On the 22nd of June, Bill and I went to dinner at his boss's house and we had a great time. Bill was sweet and kind to me the whole day. The next day, I went to the school at about 2:30 to make sure of the time. There was a beautiful bouquet of roses on the counter. (When I walked toward the secretary, she greeted me and asked me what happened to me last night. Why didn't I come to graduation? My heart sank and my legs began to shake with anger.

Your graduation is a milestone in your life that you can't retrieve. Bill robbed me of my pride that I had in myself. I graduated with honors, but it didn't matter. He had taken another happy moment in life away from me.

The next weekend was the Alumni Banquet and Dance. This is a great event in this small town where the alumni welcomed the new senior class. We stayed at my parent's house that weekend. The banquet was great although Bill had too much to drink. At this point in my life I was only drinking alone so I hadn't had anything to drink. We were dancing on the dance floor and I casually tossed a "hi" to one of the seniors from the previous year. My husband slapped me. I ran from the floor, and into his foster father. He asked me what was wrong, and I said I wasn't feeling very well. I hid for about thirty minutes, a few feet from people who were going in and out of the dance hall; I paid little attention to who they were.

Then I spotted Bill. He was looking for me. I ran and hoped that he didn't see me. I saw him get into his car and I ducked behind a building. I thought I was alone until I heard a deep voice ask me if I was okay. It was that guy that I had said hello to on the dance floor. I said I was fine, and wanted to be left alone. He grabbed my arm and I struggled. I told him that my husband was after me and that I needed to run. This guy had a real bad reputation but I knew him well enough to be certain that he would never hurt me. But I was more afraid of what my husband would do to me if he saw me talking to him. I asked him to let me go and he said that he would hide me. He was a very big guy. I saw car lights and knew that it was Bill's car. The guy told me to stand behind him so that my husband couldn't see me. My husband pulled up and yelled out the window. Who's there? The big guy yelled back at him that he had better leave him and his girlfriend alone. His huge bulk must have scared Bill away. My husband never knew that it was I hiding behind this big giant. I would never be able to repay his kindness. After Bill drove off, I thanked the guy and told him that I must go to my parent's house. He said if I should ever need anything to let him know.

Safe at home with my parents, mother came down stairs. She asked where my husband was. I couldn't tell her. I just said that I was going to meet him at the Hall in about ten minutes. She told me to be careful and to have a good time. I went back to the dance to confront him. Bill had already left town. Someone told me that he was angry and that he had gone back to our home. I saw his foster father and talked to him. I told him that I thought it was over. I explained that I couldn't handle my husband's temper any more and that it was best for me to leave him, before he got out of hand. I said nothing about the previous beatings. Bill's foster father agreed to go with me and my parent's to our house and get my things. I went back to my parent's house and told them that I was leaving him.

We got up early the next day and headed for my house to retrieve my things. I was very nervous. I wasn't sure what I would be facing when I went into the house. We pulled up to the house and my husband yelled out of the door. He said that he needed to talk to me before we started taking things out of the house. I was nervous but I knew that with my father, his foster father, and my brother outside that I would be safe.

I walked into the house. He was crying. I stood against the door because I was afraid of him. He told me that he was so very sorry for what he had done. That he didn't want to loose me. He told me that he loved me and couldn't live without me. I asked him if he had shot my dog. He bowed his head and said that he did. I hated him for that. I told him if I was to stay that things would have to change. That he was not allowed to raise his hand to my dog or me. He agreed, and I stayed. I told the men outside that I was fine and that I would be staying. They understood. Had they known that he had beaten me they would not have left me with him.

That night was quiet and uneventful. Bill's tenderness toward me was a delightful difference. But it was short lived.

Two weeks later he erupted in a rage like I had never seen before. Nothing I did was right. The dinner was cold and wasn't cooked to his liking. Again, he hit me repeatedly. Later that night we were sitting and watching TV. He looked at me and asked me a very strange question—he wanted to know if I hated him. I told him that I did. He asked what I wanted to do.

I told him that I could just call my father and have him come and get me. It was apparent that Bill feared my father and said he would just rather not be in the house when my father arrived.

Someone was really looking out for me. I was in a relationship that would assuredly escalate to the point that I wouldn't be able to survive. Bill packed his things and left. I was even more afraid than before. I called my father and he told me that my mother and he would be out to get me the next morning.

I spent the rest of the night packing my things, too afraid to sleep. I wasn't sure if Bill would change his mind and return to beat, or even kill, me. I left the next morning with mom and dad, and without looking back. Deep inside me knew that I would live with the pain of this marriage for the rest of my life. The trauma was and is to this day very painful.

People often asked me why I stayed with Bill, considering the beatings, and all. The only answer I have is fear. My fear of him was so devastating and paralyzing that he was completely in control of me. I couldn't think about the consequences of leaving him.

Bill was the type of man that feeds on his companion's low self-esteem. They beat you down emotionally, so much so that they are the only ones you feel you can turn to.

Bill would often tell me that if I ever tried to leave him that he would kill me. That fear is so very real.

Especially after you've suffered multiple beatings. You see what men (or monsters) like Bill are capable of, and their anger sends a strong message that you can't help but believe. They are potential killers.

Through his remarks, Bill made me believe that I was ugly, stupid and unlovable to anyone but him.

I agreed to Bill's request for a divorce, but I declined to go the hearing as officials told me that my presence wasn't necessary. Shortly afterwards, I received a call from Bill's lawyers telling me that the divorce wasn't going to happen unless I was present because Bill would not make an appearance. I agreed to go because I was to be remarried shortly after the divorce date.

I married Gary, one of my supervisors at the department store where I worked. Our marriage started out so wonderful. I was pregnant with our first child, and very happy. We had two children in four years. We also had four other people come into our lives. These four people were my husband's lovers.

Gary was always honest to me. He would tell me about each one of his affairs. Having the low self-esteem that I did, I would try to save our marriage through forgiveness.

One of Gary's lovers would eventually come to dinner at our home. I figured if he was going to divorce me for her—and that she was going to be a part of my children's lives—I wanted to know what she was like. She thought I was crazy for having her to dinner.

Maybe I was but I wasn't going to let this destroy me. She soon left him and he moved back in with the kids and me, until our divorce.

Our continual fondness for one another resulted in our remarriage. I was trying so hard to keep my family together I didn't realize what I was doing to myself. I began to drink heavily, and life just didn't matter. After two months we faced divorce again.

Gary said he was in love with another woman. I agreed to the divorce. But a short time later, I began to get sick. My health was failing fast. I began to hemorrhage. At first I thought I was just on my period, but after three weeks of bleeding, I saw a doctor.

I was pregnant. I thought I would die. I asked my physician why I was bleeding. An ultrasound test followed. I was pregnant with twins, and I had lost one of them. The doctor told me that I would probably loose the other one by six months.

The divorce was hard on my pregnancy. Five months into my pregnancy, I began having migraine headaches.

The doctor was sure I would loose the baby, so he did everything he could for me. He agreed to administer medication for the headaches, even though there was a great risk to my baby. At eight months into the pregnancy I came down with chicken pox. At this point, there was tremendous concern that the baby would be severely deformed or retarded. My son was born in August, and he was perfect. There seemed to be nothing wrong with him.

I went back to work one week after I had the baby. I collapsed at work, and I was hemorrhaging again. I was diagnosed with uterine displaitia. I would have to go in to have an emergency hysterectomy. I was told that I would die without the treatment. There was no choice.

While in the hospital, Gary told me he was going to remarry. This woman would be his last girl friend. I was bed ridden for six weeks. A friend came to stay with me during this time.

One day I received a call from Gary's fiance'. She asked me if I would be her bride's maid. I told her that I would me delighted. I knew that it was just a mind game she was playing. She wanted me to know that Gary was no longer going to be mine. I never knew until later how much of a hold I really had on this man. I was glad that he would be out of my life. I needed to move on. However, I would not move on for two and a half years.

Gary had crushed my life, my world. All I wanted to do is die. I wrote many things in my journal. Most of them depressing and macabre. I talked of suicide, but yet they all said, like a promise to some unseen being, that I would go on living—if only for my children. Harry will always be a part of my life; we share three wonderful children. This chapter of my life will never be over, only different from day to day.

I quit working for the department store. My sister had a friend that got us both jobs at a delivery company. We were delivering pharmaceuticals to stores. I loved being a driver. Dave our boss was terrific. When he gave me the driving test he asked me why I wanted to be a driver. I simply replied that I didn't. I thought that he was going to give me a job in the office. I was too afraid to tell him because I needed the job. The boss, my sister and I got real close. He needed someone in the office eventually so he asked me to be his secretary. I said yes. I thought it might be a promotion or a raise. I ended up working 48 hours per week and only getting paid for 20 hours. At the time it was okay. I loved working for Dave and we became real close. I could talk to him about everything. I started dating one of the drivers shortly after I was moved into the office. This relationship would not last. Jeff was very self centered and began to walk all over me. However, I was not the one who ended the relationship.

ANOTHER MAN

$\mathcal{I}$ WAS WORKING FOR the delivery company when I met John. He was one of the pharmacists that I delivered to. I didn't deliver to him often, but the second time that I did he told me that he was also a stockbroker. Well I had some stock and I needed to get rid of it. So the next time that I saw John I told him my telephone number. I asked him if he would check it out and let me know what I can do. I asked him if we could talk about it over dinner or something. That was on a Friday. I had no idea that he would really call me back. He was a very handsome man and he seemed a little out of my league.

He seemed to be very intelligent, too. I wasn't sure if could hold up my end of the conversation.

That night my sister Ann and I were caring for her daughter and sister Fae's kids, plus three of my own. We had a house full. Fae returned earlier than expected, but the kids wanted to stay over. To make the evening complete, we rented movies and made popcorn.

About mid-evening the phone rang. It was John. At first I didn't know what to think. We talked for a while and he seemed very nice. He had called to see what night I was free to have dinner with him. His schedule was much more complex than mine was, so I suggested that he pick a day. He said Thursday was best for him.

Then, out of politeness, I asked him to consider coming over for coffee before he began his trip home in the mountains. I was certain that he would decline and request a "rain check." I was surprised when he said that was a great idea and asked for directions.

After giving John some rather sketchy guidance to my house, I rushed downstairs and asked my sisters if it was okay. She thought it was a wonderful idea.

An hour later, the doorbell rang, it was John. My heart pounded. I was so nervous I was shaking. Wasting no time, we drove to the Broker, a posh restaurant, and enjoyed shrimp cocktails. Then, it was on to the Warf to dance.

We must have stared at each other for hours without saying a word. In a short time I learned a lot about John. His wife, Mary, had died the previous year of heart failure at 29. I could tell that he loved her dearly, and I could see that he was still not over the pain of losing her.

He told me more about why he was a pharmacist and a stockbroker. I believed that John was going to be very wealthy some day. I wasn't wrong. Then he told me about his plan for his future. Within five years he would "own the world." His scheme was fabulous, and I knew that if any one could do it, he could.

John and I dated for two or three months. During that time we both grew. We loved each other's company and we always had a good time. At one point however, I knew I couldn't compete with his dead wife. I was falling in love with this man and knew I would never have his love completely. I was frightened and shared my fears with him.

He told me that I was right; he could never love anyone the way he loved Mary. We went our separate ways, though we remain friends to this day. By the way, John has become fabulously wealthy, and he still lives in Colorado. I don't hear from him any more, but I know he's found peace with Mary. And I wish him the very best.

Looking back, I recall a conversation that we had. I told John that I had always wanted to become a police officer. He said that he could see me in that line of work, but not as a hardcore cop. He also told me that he believed that if I became a law officer, I would blow my brains out within six months. I believe he was probably right. That is the main reason I never went through with becoming a police officer. I was unstable and didn't realize it. I thank the Lord that a friend saw this and told me. I believe that people come into life for a reason. This relationship was very special. I was able to help a very dear friend through a very difficult time. Don't ever pass up the chance to help another human being. Give of yourself and expect nothing in return. The Lord will reward you for the kindness you show to others.

I sabotaged this relationship. I now know that if I had given John time to heal we may have had a great life together. But at that time in my life I had a lot of healing to do myself. However, I felt that I needed a man to make me happy and to take care of me. I am a very caring person and I love to take care of others. I didn't know that then, and I wouldn't realize it for years. Also, I couldn't comprehend that it's okay to have someone take care of you when you need it.

I always seemed to be looking for that magical relationship. I saw that closeness in each person that I dated. Then when it didn't work out, I would only blame myself. I thought that there had to be something wrong with me. I could never hold on to a man. I would date three others in a course of a year. I thought each time that I would marry and live happily ever after. They all proposed marriage, and I said yes to them all. Nonetheless, the weddings never came about. They would find someone else and move on.

When I met Tim, it was a breath of fresh air. But this would prove to be a very dangerous relationship for me. All of my beliefs would go out the window. This was a man that I fell for instantly. He could get me to do things that I would have never done and shouldn't have done. Tim was a user and it took me many years to figure that out. He didn't believe in God and he tried to make me believe that there wasn't life beyond this world. He questioned the word of God, and, unfortunately, I started to believe him.

We drank every night. Sometimes all day, too. Tim entered me into a corset contest. That means very little clothing. I got drunk and walked down the runway with very little on. I won the contest, but felt very dirty with all the drunks yelling at me. I hated myself once again. As the editor of a semi-porn newspaper, Steven made me Miss January. To this day it's hard for me to realize I let him take such a revealing photograph of me.

Finally, I got fed up with this destructive relationship after a night of drinking. I started to go out dancing every night. In the course of my slide, I met many people, some where great and others were not. I stopped drinking when I went out. I guess I realized that the bottom of a bottle was not where I wanted to be anymore. Tim and I spent a lot of time together.

One weekend, we went water skiing at Bony Reservoir. We had a great time, even though I became too drunk to stand. I was joking around and grabbed a big butcher knife and slammed it on the picnic table, my hand slipped and slid down the knife. I quickly put an adhesive bandage on it and told everyone that it was just a small cut.

The next morning I woke up all sticky. The shirt I was wearing was covered with blood. My hand was throbbing. I pulled off the small bandage and could see the bone of my finger.

Covering the wound again, I left the tent and told Tim that my hand hurt. He told me he would get me some ice. He opened up the cooler and the water was red with blood. There was blood every where. The picnic table, the butter, the sour cream. Everything was covered in blood. Tim wanted to take me to the hospital. I refused to go. I told him I was fine and to hand me the bourbon. I took the all too familiar two swigs and told my brother that I was ready to go skiing. It was hard to hold on the rope but I had to prove to every one that I was just fine and didn't need to go to any hospital. I was lucky; I could have cut my finger off. It could have gotten very infected with the alkali water in the lake. But again God was with me.

I'll never forget the night I met Joe and Peter. They were nice. Joe, unlike Peter, was married. Peter and I talked for hours. He was dealing with his mother's death from cancer. He told me wonderful stories about the great lady, and said that he was to inherit quit a lot of money in the next few months. A generous man, he wanted to share with everyone.

The next thing I knew Peter was living with me and I couldn't quite figure out how that happened. It just did, and I didn't resist it.

Peter took me to see the house that he was to inherit. It was huge. I had always wanted a house of my own.

I began to get sick again, but, as customary, I wouldn't see a doctor to find out what was wrong with me. I would get sick with almost every one of my relationships. I felt like I was dying. I needed to take care of my kids and at this time two of my kids just couldn't deal with the barrage of men coming and going. They wanted to live with their father. I couldn't blame them. Between my sisters and me there were lots of men.

I couldn't let go of my youngest, though. Lee was my baby. After my kids were gone I went into a deep depression. Their father sent me a form to sign. He said it was for his insurance. He lied, or I was too depressed to know it, but I was signing away my rights to my kids. I didn't realize this until it was too late. I suffered a nervous breakdown after signing those papers, not thinking that he would do anything like that to me at my weakest moment.

I married Peter and got worse physically. Things started to become cloudy. My niece, Cathy, was failing in school and her mother, Fae, asked if she could come and live with me. I told her she could. At this time my sister Fae was living out of her car because her latest boyfriend had taken all of her money and she didn't have a job. Despite her dilemma, she didn't ask me to assume responsibility for her other two girls.

I took custody of Cathy. Her grades changed dramatically. She made the honor role and I was so very proud of her. However, Fae became angry about this. She blamed me for coming between her and her daughter, insisting that her daughter move back with her.

Cathy didn't want to go back to that life. I called her father and told him what was going on and thought that it be better for his daughter if he took over custody of her. My sister was furious with me, but it was the best for this child. Cathy had succeeded at something and continues to do so. Her father came into town within two days and had my sister sign over custody to him. It was for the best. My sister didn't talk to me for about three months, but her life was in turmoil and she soon forgot about Cathy. Out of sight out of mind.

While leaving work one night, Peter and I were waived over by the police as we were leaving the parking lot. I was confident that I hadn't done anything wrong. The officer asked if Peter was in the car with me. I said yes, and they asked Peter to get out of the car. Moments later, Peter was in handcuffs.

I asked what was going on, but they wouldn't tell me. I asked Peter what he wanted me to do. He told me nothing. I drove home and looked through some of his things. He had a little shoe box full of papers and a phone book. I started to call his family. I was so very surprised to hear them say that they had not talked to him in years and wanted to keep it that way. This was very unsettling. According to the stories that he had told me he was supposed to be racing his brother in-law's car in two weeks. He had been fitted for a fire suit and was very excited about the sponsors that they were racing for. He called that night and told me to call his grandmother. He said that she would bail him out the next day. I asked him about what his family said to me. He made up something and I believed him. Of course my mind was not thinking straight either. I called his grandmother and she told me that if I would pick her up at her house that we would go down together and get him out.

I still had no explanation as to why Peter was jailed. His grandmother was frail and close to ninety-six years old. She told me that she was glad that he had found someone to take care of him because she wouldn't be around much longer. We arrived at the courthouse earlier than expected, so over coffee she told me about her daughter, Peter's mother. I was puzzled at what she was saying. She talked about her as if she were still alive. I couldn't bring myself to ask her what she was talking about. I thought that maybe she simply hadn't accepted the death of her daughter. She told me that Peter was a good kid, just misunderstood.

She bailed him out with her life savings, $2,600. When we dropped her at her house she said goodbye and kissed us both. I later asked Peter why she acted as if his mother was still alive. He excused her actions, saying that she was merely old and couldn't accept the fact of her daughter's death.

The next day we walked into a department store. He went one way and I the other. When I went to the register I was baffled. I looked at the women behind the counter and was shocked to see the woman Peter had shown me photos of . . . his mother.

With barely enough nerve, I asked her name. She told me her name (and reaffirmed my suspicions). I said, "Do you know that you're supposed to be dead?"

She was puzzled at what I said, and remarked that she was fine. At last, I announced that I was her daughter in-law, and that her son, Peter, had informed me that she was dead.

At that point, Peter came to the counter. I stared at him and exclaimed, "Look, your mother has had a remarkable recovery, she's back from the dead!" With that, I left the store as quickly as I could.

Peter followed me without saying a word to his "dead" mother. That night, I kicked him out and retreated to my parent's house. They were frightened for me and called the Colorado Health Center to inquire about Peter.

A Center official advised them not to let me go back home. They said that Peter was a pathological liar and now that I'd backed him into the corner with truths, he might become violent. I stayed with my parents for three days. Long enough for Peter to find an apartment and remove his things from my house.

But that wasn't the end of my problems with Peter. He phoned me repeatedly. At one point, I had to call the police to report him because he was at my door and wouldn't leave.

I called Steven and told him what had happened and told him I needed to get out of here for a while. He took me to a motel and we spent three days there. I called my parents and told them I was okay, but I just needed to stay away from my house for a while; they agreed that it was a good idea. They kept my son, Lee, for me and asked no questions as to where I was.

I saw a lawyer and he asked me what I wanted to do. He advised me that I could commit Peter or divorce him. If I had him committed, I wouldn't be able to divorce him for seven years. I chose to divorce him. Then it hit me. I knew nothing about this man I called my husband. The lawyer asked me his date of birth. I didn't know, I didn't know anything about him. When I met Peter I had no idea how sick he really was. He had lived to that point in lies for over ten years. He lied about his mother being dead, and the money that she had supposedly left him. The two Corvettes that he claimed to own and the racing job, all lies. He said that he had been married before and had a two-year son that he wasn't allowed to see. I never found out if that was the truth or not, but I believe now that it was another lie.

Peter was a very good liar. He said that he had talked to a salesman at a Chevrolet dealership about a truck for me. I had always wanted a truck. I even saw the truck. The dealership had it custom-detailed with pinstripes and my name on it. Now, a dealership won't do something like that without someone paying for the unit, or at least depositing money on the sale. Like I said, Peter knew how to lie. That's how he got through life. He pulled people in by convincing them that he would take care of them financially, as soon as his inheritance came through. His plan would have worked on me, too, had I not accidentally discovered his mother, or called his family the night he went to jail.

One day, I was painting a window advertisement for a business friend of my father's when a very handsome man approached me. He said is name was Eric and that he was opening up a karate school nearby and needed his windows painted.

A few hours later, I bid the job for $1,200. Tony accepted and asked me to start the following Monday. Well, I ended up painting more that I figured and adjusted my price by $1000.00. That's when things got real screwed up.

I began dating Tony and was eventually offered a job by his brother, Lee, in California. I would never guess what was in store for me and Lee. But it was California or bust.

We lived in a beautiful house where all of our needs were met. Tony had a lot of music equipment and was very worried that Lee might damage it. Tony would lock Lee in his room at night and then spank him for wetting his bed.

Tony's children were with us also and I soon realized the hate these kids had for their dad. Then I figured out why. He was abusive. He would lock his kids out of the house and call them stupid. Tony held five black belts in various martial arts and I was afraid he might practice on me.

My father had begged me not to go with him, he even cried, something I never saw my father do. However, children don't always listen to their parents. In some ways, that's because they can't comprehend that parents might know something about love. When a parent tells you not to take a certain course of action, it's probably because—first and foremost—they love you, and, secondly, you're probably thinking with your heart and, perhaps, not thinking straight.

Now, let's think about what I'm asking you to do. Listen, listen, and listen. Just as you want your parents to listen to you, you need to listen to them, too. Parents are looking out for you. Sometimes, it's hard for them to let you go. Give them time. Also, parents need to have a little more faith in what they've taught you to this point. Also as teenagers you need to have a little more faith in your parents. Maybe they do know what they are talking about. However, parents are human and make mistakes just like you do. Let them make theirs and they'll let you make yours.

The final straw was when Tony wanted to spank Lee for doing something one of his kids did. I argued with Tony, and he struck me in the face. With a shattered nose, I ran to the bathroom to get some tissues, but Tony grabbed me and pushed me back into a chair.

Lee and I left the next day, leaving all of my worldly possessions behind. We were lucky to get out of that place with the clothes on our backs, and our lives. Tony was a dangerous man . . . a weapon that knew how to hit you without leaving any bruises. Leaving wasn't our best choice; it was our only choice.

When we got back to Colorado, I was able to have my other two children visit me. They stayed for one week. It was so wonderful. I didn't want them to leave.

However, I had signed away my rights to them. Their father, Gary, came to pick them up on a Sunday.

Monday afternoon, I received a phone call from Gary. He told me that the kids didn't want to live with him any longer and that I should come and get them. I had him sign them back over to me and I took my kids home to live.

I worked at a 50's and 60's club where I had been a frequent patron. It was a part-time job and got me out of the house.

I loved to dance and when the manager asked me to audition I was flattered. During this time I entered another relationship, and, once again, a man moved into my apartment before I realized what was happening.

Ken was much younger than I and acted it. He had a lot of growing to do. He also had a hard time with my kids and me having to deal with my ex-husband, Gary. Ken left one day and I still didn't know whether he's dead or alive.

It was a Friday night when one of the bar managers told me how sorry he was that things hadn't worked out between Ken and me. Perplexed, I asked him what he was talking about. He said that he had learned from Ken that day that he was in Missouri and he wouldn't be returning to work at the bar.

Needless to say I was extremely upset. I brushed it off, though, and returned to work. While I was walking through the bar, one of the regular customers asked me if I was okay. I said, "Yes, why?" He said that I looked unhappy. I explained what had happened upset and that I just couldn't talk about it anymore. He told me that if I needed to talk that he was there for me. I thanked him and went to work.

While dancing a solo number, a regular customer approached me and asked me to dance with him. I told him I didn't want to, remembering that the last time we were on the floor together he threw me in the air and caught me, bruising my ribs.

Finally, I agreed to dance with him if he promised that he wouldn't put me through aerial maneuvers. He willingly complied, but the next thing I knew I was in the air bourn again. This time I made a perfect landing, but when he pulled me under his arm his elbow made contact with my nose and smashed it.

He patted me on the back and reassured me that I would be fine—I was just going to bleed a little. I screamed obscenities at him and told him that he broke my nose. My brother was in the bar at the time and he rushed over to me. The DJ yelled over the loud speakers for help, and it seemed as though everyone responded. What a way to end an evening.

I was rushed to the hospital and given a name of a plastic surgeon. Here I was: two black eyes, a broken nose, and a broken heart. I received a phone call that next day from the customer that had asked me ". . . if I was okay?" He had heard what had happened and begged my manager for my phone number. When he asked if I needed anything, I told him that all I needed was company; I was going stir-crazy because I wasn't going to be seen in public with bandages on my eyes and nose.

His name was Steve. He came over that day to care of my kids and me. He told me that he was going over to his parent's house and wondered if I wanted to go. I didn't really want to go, but it was better than staying at home. His parents were so gracious and they never said anything about my eyes or my nose. The kids had a great time and, frankly, so did I.

That was April 7, 1990. We were married six months later. It was a magical wedding. We had goals and dreams and each other.

My niece, Cathy, moved back to Colorado with her husband and we all became very close. We went everywhere together. It seemed every one we knew wanted to have a relationship like Steve and I. Some wanted to be our friends so that they could be around two people that genuinely loved each other. Our enchanting time would last eight years.

The youngest of my sister's girls, Kelly, had just graduated from high school. She was coming out to visit. We were all excited about her arrival. We had great fun with showing her the city. We watched movies and ate popcorn and laughed.

About two weeks into her visit I noticed that there was something different. Something just wasn't right.

Steve stopped talking to me. I asked him what was wrong and he had no reply. He looked depressed and sad most of the time. The only time that he was not sad was when my Kelly entered the room. At first I thought that it was just that he didn't want to ruin her visit, but my woman's intuition wouldn't let it alone.

Before leaving on a business trip, I left Steve a note pleading with him to please tell me what was going on when I returned. We were able to talk about anything up to that point; however, that communication was all gone now.

When I returned home on schedule, Steve wasn't there, by choice, I'm sure. I guess I knew that our relationship wasn't going to last, mostly because he didn't want it to. I'd been home about an hour when he walked in. He said we needed to talk, then led me to the bedroom and sat me down. He then told me that he was leaving me. He told me that it was because he couldn't stand Lee, my youngest son. I couldn't believe what I was hearing. After eight wonderful years of marriage and raising my three kids, he decided that he could no longer be married to me because of a child. I asked him to tell me the truth. I asked him if it had anything to do with my niece Kelly. He said that it didn't and that they were just close friends. Deep down, I knew that he was lying. I knelt down to pray. I asked God to show me why this was happening to me again.

Eventually, Steve and I talked about the last two months and how during that time we had made love. I had also told Cathy about that. She in turn told her sister, Kelly, with whom my husband had left me for. He asked if I would call Kelly and tell her that I had lied about having sex with him. I asked him if he wanted me to do this because he wanted to continue his relationship with Kelly or if the lie would make life any easier for him to explain what he had done. He told me that there was nothing going on between Kelly and him. I then told him what God had put in my heart. I told him that he had taken many things from me in the last three months, my heart and my peace and he had destroyed my family. He had betrayed not only me but also my children. I told him that I had nothing to be ashamed of. All I had done was make love to my husband and I wasn't about to let him take the only thing I had left, my dignity.

Then Steve said something that finalized everything. He said: "If you don't want me to hate you, you will tell this lie." I asked him to leave and told him that I would not lie to anyone. I had nothing to hide.

After Steve was gone I knew I had done the right thing. The Lord filled me with peace and I began to heal.

Rumors began to fly throughout my family about Steve and Kelly getting married and having children that I was unable to give him, a son of his own. I stopped living, I stopped eating and sleeping. It took Four years for the divorce to be final. During the first six months I lost seventy-five pounds. I again began to cope with tragedy. Lee was hurt the most. His rage was beyond anything I had ever seen. His teachers were worried and so was I. I somehow managed to forgive Steve and Kelly for their betrayal, but my kids weren't able to pardon either of them. To this day they carry that with them.

To be betrayed by someone you love isn't easy to recover from. I've learned from my past that if you don't forgive others for the hurt that they may cause you, it will just eat you up inside. I guess I have always looked at life as a journey. We can learn and move on or choose not to.

If God can forgive us, why shouldn't we forgive each other? Two of my sisters have never been able to forgive people that have hurt them and they are not very nice people to be around. They have one rough time after another, and can never seem to get ahead in life. I believe that they never will, at least until they start forgiving those who have hurt them in one way or another.

My question to you now is, do you need to forgive anyone? If you do, I pray that you will do this soon. You'll be amazed at the freedom this will give you in your life. We are only human, we all make mistakes, and we all have choices. Please forgive others and do it not for them, but for you. Let God guide your life. Everything is in His timing, not yours. You may want things back the way they were, but He has a better plan for you. Trust in God, let Him guide you. Have faith. There are no accidents. God's placed you here for a reason. He may want you to learn something or He may need you to teach someone else. You just need to trust Him. He'll not steer you in the wrong direction. Only we take the wrong road. Remember He loves you. There are no guarantees in life. You can't make someone love you if they don't want to. The only person you can change is yourself. When something like this happens to you, look to God for help. He and only He can ease the pain learn from the experience. Become a better person than you are right now. Don't let someone take away your dignity. You know what's right, even if the other person doesn't. They may destroy your family and break your heart, but don't let them rob you of your faith.

It's really funny when you watch people. Mothers mostly. Some moms baby their kids when they get hurt they help them to feel better. Some could really care less. They watch their kids and watch them just waiting for them to do something wrong. Then they pounce on them. They seem to want to prove to people in public that they discipline them in a harsh way. The children don't really understand but what can they do? Nothing.

As you look at them closely, you'll find that a mother may be well dressed while her child's in rags. Why don't they care about them? Why don't they care what their children look like? They take such pride in what they have on? There's nothing you can do, because they aren't your children; they don't belong to you.

This was a thought that I had when I was in my early twenties. A lot has changed since then. You can make a difference in the lives of children, even if they aren't your own. I used to dream about being the neighborhood mom. You know the place where all the kids hang out. I wanted my children to be proud of me. I wanted them to want to hang out with me.

Well, my dream's come true. I am the neighborhood mom, and all of my children are proud of me and want to be around me. I have approximately twenty-three children, including my own three children. I've heard kids say to others that I am the "coolest mom ever." I have had parents call me to thank me for being there for their kids. They tell me that their kids won't talk to them. The parents try to get through, but they can't get past that wall that teenagers put up. I think this is true of most teenagers. They just can't see themselves talking to their parents about their personal lives, like if a boy breaks a girl's heart, or a girl breaks a boy's heart. They can't talk to their parents about that. The thing parents try to tell their kids is that they were young once and they know what they're going through.

I know that my kids don't always tell me everything, but their friends do. After talking to these kids I've realized that the difference is that I sit and listen. That's all; I never give them advice unless they ask for it. In most cases they ask me what I think they should do. I tell them I can't answer that, but I can let you know what I'd do. I also try to let them see the other person's side of it. Another thing: I don't judge them. It's not my place to judge anyone. Parents try to fix their kids. Sometimes as parents we forget how lonely it was when we where young. We forget the feeling of how nice it would be if someone would just stop and listen to what he or she is saying. Kids worry a lot about how others will view them. The last thing they need is to be viewed by their own parents as something other than the standards that we all hold our kids to.

Parenting doesn't come with a manual or guidelines. We all go at it blindly. We just need to teach our children right from wrong and when they become teenagers pray that it's enough to help them make the right choices. When they don't make the right choices, we must let them know that even though they made a bad choice, we still love them . . . unconditionally

Back when I was young and dreaming about being the Neighborhood Mom, I had no idea how challenging and rewarding it would be. The thing that was so scary to me was that I was being listened to. Kids were listening to what I had to say. That meant that I had to choose my words carefully. The last thing I needed was to have some child take what I said and use it to hurt someone. So I came up with the only thing I could. Listen, listen, listen and then listen some more. Then let them make their own decisions. I believe that most parents do a good job in teaching their kids right from wrong. All I do is bring that out in them.

So, when you think that you can't make a difference in your community, think again. Take the time to listen. To date, I've taken four teenagers into my home. Their parents, for one reason or another, kicked them out. The youngest was fifteen, the oldest eighteen.

Sally, the youngest of my "adopted" children, made a bad choice. She lied to me and lost her safe haven—I only ask that "my" kids not lie to me. Because of her falsehood, I sent her back home to her mother, where her mother shipped her off to whatever relative that would take her. When Sally returned to Colorado, I allowed her to move back in. Sally never lied to me again. She said that she would do anything to get my trust back. She began to make choices, set goals, and dared to dream about the future, but not for long.

Sally eventually returned to live with her mother and, unfortunately, reverted to telling lies. I pray for her, that she will not destroy her life.

I've dedicated a wall in my home just for pictures of my wonderful children. Some of them are going to college, some have moved out of state. Others are now engaged to be married. They'll be fine, I know, and they all know that my home is their home.

Never look at the obvious. There are more grays in life than any other color. I believe that there are no blacks and whites in life. We all seek love, life, and the pursuit of happiness. However, we all see things differently. You can't and won't ever know what another is thinking or feeling. You may have gone through the same thing but you react to things differently than anyone else. All we can hope is to ease the pain of others by being there for them and listening to them. Whether they need to vent or cry to be a true friend is to just be there for them. Remember God gave us two ears and only one mouth.

THE SPIRAL

$\mathscr{T}$HE SPIRAL, WHAT IS it. When looking back at my life and the lives of other members of my family, I have noticed a spiral effect. When looking at my life I can see with every tragedy I recover great. I become very proud of myself and become strong. People will tell me that they don't know how I made it through my trials. They say they wouldn't be able to recover so completely or strongly. This part of the spiral is great. My self-esteem grows and I feel great. It may take me one year or even two to recover. However, when I do, I am admired by those who think they would not recover so gracefully. After hearing so many congratulate me it's almost as if I get conceded or full of myself. When this happens I guess I get cocky. I began to expect more from everyone where I am concerned. I expect men to buy me the drinks and expect men to see only me in a bar. A friend of mine had only one description of this. "The Blond Phase." I become what I hate most: "A dumb blond."

When I realize that no one is talking to me again and they don't want to be around me, I crash. My self-esteem drops. I feel as if I don't deserve the very best that life has to give. I start to settle for whatever I can get. A man may ask me out in this period and I will say yes, just to have a date, even though I know in my heart that he's all wrong for me. Even if I know this man may beat me, I'll date him. If I get trapped in a negative relationship (with no hope of escape) I discover that partner may feed on my low self-esteem, picking at what dignity I may have left.

They often control you at first with words, then with anger and fear. Before too long you feel worthless. You sense that you don't deserve to live. At thirty-eight, I've managed to recover from even the worst of situations.

Still, other family members aren't that fortunate. Some have continued to fall deeper into the spiral. Alcohol, drug, sex have become their best allies. Friends of destruction. Then suicide seems the only way out of the spiral. If it hadn't been for a very dear friend, I wouldn't have seen it.

Her name was Joyce. She was very apprehensive about talking to me, but I thank God she did. She saw that my mind became scattered. I was unable to focus on even small tasks at work. I was making many mistakes that I had never done before. When Joyce approached me, she said she understands what it means to be a dumb blonde. A term she would never use when talking to or about me. When she told me what she saw, I was able to take a long hard look at myself. She told me that the prettier I got, the dumber I became. That the more compliments I got the worse the spiral got.

When I took a step back for a better look at what she was saying, I was sure that Joyce was crazy. I was angry with her. I had decided that she was not my friend at all. Nevertheless, I was able to see the truth in her message at times.

I began to see the mistakes I was making and correct them, I took responsibility for those mistakes and that helped me to recover. I became the model employee again; my kids began to mind and respect me. Once, I came far enough out of the spiral to reflect back into my life; I saw that with every heartfelt tragedy I went through, I began this spiral. I'd get myself into a bad relationship, and really have a bad tragedy. Or, as I like to put it, another chapter in my "Book of Life."

Joyce saw the change in me. She told me that she had thought she had lost me forever. She didn't think I'd ever be able to have the self-confidence again or the self-esteem. She asked me what I did to change thing almost over night. I had to tell her that once she had brought it to my attention; I could reflect on what was happening and stop thinking of myself as a dumb blonde. I'd hate to think what would have happened if she had said nothing. Or where I would be today. She told me that I should be so very proud of myself for growing in myself enough to realize what was happening. Or what I was doing, not only myself, but to my children.

Each day someone reinforces this in my past. After fourteen years, I saw Tim, a former boyfriend of my sister, Ann. He was amazed at the person I had become.

As we reminisced about the wild days we all had together, I could see the pattern of the spiral so very clearly. I had always tried to forget the past. It was too painful, but when talking to someone I had just met, I would always bring these tragedies in my life up. I needed someone to feel sorry for me or I needed that compliment to give me that fix of "you're wonderful, you're beautiful."

Now when I'm complimented by a man (or woman), I feel wonderful and secretly say to myself, "I know." Then I stop and do something intellectually. Something that will reinforce what I've deeply known all along . . . that I'm more than beauty. I'm a warm, intelligent, caring, giving human being. I'm more that just a man's plaything. I'm okay with being just me. I don't need the accolades to feel worth while. Each time a man proposes to me nowadays, I laugh. I don't have to say yes, because I fear being alone forever. Or, so what if I'm lonely? I don't have to be. I have God and my kids. They all love me, even with my faults.

I've begun to heal after many years of destroying myself. Now, I am able to share these wonderful discoveries about life's little ups and downs with others. Look deep within yourself, I say. Find that person you think you can be. You can be this person. You just need to see life for what it really is. God put us here to flourish. He doesn't make any junk. You are a worthwhile person; you do deserve the very best.

Once you begin to believe in yourself, there will be many, many bumps along the way. Remember, stop, do something that makes you feel good about yourself. I mean you, not him, not her, not them, but you, and only you. You were smart enough to read this book, to find some hope. The power's really within you. I believe you can do it. If I did, you can. Call a support group; talk about how you feel how others make you feel. Don't judge yourself or others while doing this. The act of speaking these things out loud will make all the difference in the world. Don't talk about these things to your partner if you have any reason to believe you're in a negative relationship. He or she won't understand. They'll want to fix you, and they may even assume that you're blaming them, even though you may not be. You may be venting your feeling, but they aren't going to understand this.

I urge you to find someone who can understand this. Talk with someone to whom you can say, "Don't try to fix me; I just need to vent and talk or even ramble about something. I don't want your opinion; I just need a sounding board. I am the one who needs to figure this out. Don't even give me suggestions. Just hold me when I need to cry, tell me that I'm going to be okay, and by all means, don't think me crazy. Don't repeat any of this to any one."

Some day that person will need you to do the same. I also believe that you'll discover at some point, they'll tell you that they've felt the same, or can relate to what you're saying. You'll find that this true friend will become your one-person support group. The two of you will learn from each other. Just know that no one's right and no one's wrong. All you're doing is talking and not trying to figure it out. There'll come a time when you'll figure it out. That's when you'll experience a great sense of accomplishment and an overwhelming freedom within.

Before you begin to talk with your friend, sit down and say a prayer. Ask God to guide you, to help you to be open, no matter what comes out of your mouth. Even if you have never prayed before you'll be amazed how much this will help.

My friend, Joyce, and I have learned over this past year that we talk out loud and we can not only just vent, but, we can grow as women. I've since started other discussions with male friends, not to the same degree, but nonetheless small portions. What this has taught me is the other side of the coin. You can get a man's point of view with out asking for it. My suggestion is still not to have these talks with your spouse. Some of the things you need to talk about will be about him. This also teaches men a little bit more about how women are and what they need.

I also suggest finding out more about the man you married or involved with. You may have been married to him for many years but do you know why he does the things he does? Do you know why some things he does really makes you made? You need to first find out what personality you are. What makes you tick? Then find out what makes your partner tick. Read personality books like, "Personality Plus" by Florence Littauer, "Positive Personality Profiles" and "Who Do You Think You Are Anyway" by Robert A. Rohm,

Ph.D. Other great books to read are "Dynamic People Skills" by Dexter Yeager, "Seeds of Greatness" by Dennis Whaitly, and of course. "The Bible".

For much of my life I've never been able to read very long without falling asleep. That's changed. I can read for hours on end now. I've found that when you start to learn who you are and the people around you are, it opens up so many possibilities. It gives you a greater understanding of the human race.

I've come to realize that I have a gift for helping others. It makes me happy to help others to understand why things are happening to them. However, in my own life I've never been able to help myself. Things are becoming clearer for me know.

I've been diagnosed with PTSD (post traumatic stress). Now that I'm on medication, I can see things that have happened in my life and figured some of them out. Yet, there'll always be trials; I understand that. I also know that I can do all things through God that strengthens me. Get to know god. Once you have a personal relationship with God you'll know true peace.

Thoughts in Poetry

In this section, I'm presenting poems that I've written during these dark times in my life. I understand that they may not mean much to some as they have me, nevertheless, I want to share them with you as they show my desperate call for help. At the bottom of some of my writings, I've placed notes beneath some to further explain what I was referring to.

Behind bars

I want to be free.
I want to try.
If I can not be,
I want to die.

Written in the memory of my brother, Wayne. He was always trying to be free of the problems that plague many teenagers.

What Can I Do?

What can I do?
My life is jumbled.
For have I a friend in the world?
Can I ever live my life the way?
I want it to be lived?
The questions I ask, can they be answered?
Or do I have to keep loving someone; I do love, but
    not enough to marry?
Must I pretend?

Written after my first husband beat me in my parent's house.

People

The people that surround me, do they care?
The ones I love will they let me be free,
The way I want to be free?
I can't tell them I love them, but yet
I can't take my love away from them,
For fear of hurting them so badly.
It would kill me.
You see, my story starts with pain
But they don't get or feel the pain
I do

Written after one of my suicide attempts: I took fifty aspirin.

Forget The Love

The love and laughter I see everyday are the tears I
    may cry tomorrow.
People pass by and I start to wonder why.
They seem to forget that I was once their friend
They have forgotten the love
And the care that I had once given them in their time
    of need.
Those who choose to forget the love will someday
    remember the hate.

Written after one of my many friendships crumbled. It
was hard for me to keep close friends. They got in the
way. They couldn't get too close or they discover my
secrets.

It's My Life

It's my life, and I have so many questions to ask,
But can anyone answer them?
No. At least I doubt it.
Some people think I'm crazy because of the poems I
    write.
I don't care.
My poems may not make much sense to them, but
    they do to me.
I shall do as my heart tells me.
The life I have inside of me,
Is the death I hold for tomorrow.
The ones I love now will soon be hurt.
For I love too many.
The pleasure I had wished I had is the pleasure I had,
    but lost in love.
The friends I have now will be strangers in Hell.
Although in friendship it takes but one lie.

Written the day before another suicide attempt. I was
lying to my friends and couldn't deal with the lies. I
wanted to please everyone and yet ended up losing
everyone and everything that I held dear.

How

How can I cope with the pain?
How can I forget the memory?
How can I live without him?
How do I know if he still cares?
How can I tell?
How can I stop the pain pulling at my stomach?
How can I be able to live?
I still love him?

Written after my brother's death. I couldn't let go and I didn't understand that I really didn't need to let go. My parents were so hurt and sad I couldn't add to their pain and ask a lot of dumb questions. I now know that I could have and should have asked those questions. Questions are good and helpful. They can help the person asking and the one who is trying to answer. Not all questions can be answered, but by talking about things it will help both parties.

Someday

I wait the day.
That day in which my life may change completely.
Eight days and another year will pass.
The memories of the past, the hard times and happy
    moments.
The friends I've had and lost and the people I await to
    meet.
The understanding of my friends.
And all I have to ask is . . . will I ever truly understand
    them?

My friends were trying to understand the pain that I
was going through. However, the things they would
say were so painful. They still had their brothers. Even
after a year the pain didn't diminish.

Pain

It's been five years since it happened.
Why can't I forget or at least stop the hurting?
The loss I have inside me is a loss that I can't forget.
He was my brother.
Why must I pay for someone else's mistakes?
Why must I pay for the bullet that went through his
  brain?
Will it ever stop hurting?
Will I ever forget?

While writing this, I was torn between not wanting
the hurt and not wanting to forget what my brother
gave me. I was angry that I thought that I had to
choose. You don't have to choose. I now remember
him with fond memories and happy times we spent
together.

Find

The hate I have inside of me is
The fear I shall await.
The love I once had for this person
Is the hate I have now for him?
The fear I have is not for me, but for
The people around me.
For which of them may I
Fall in love with next.

I had a terrible fear of hurting people. I felt that everything and everyone I loved, I destroyed. I blamed myself for so many tragedies that happened. Not just to me but to the people around me.

Winning and Losing

It seems I just can't win.
I loose everything.
Love, people, and life.
Why do people say things that aren't true?
I try my best to make friends,
But every time I get close to someone they seem to
    disappear.
When will I ever win?
Is the love of my life the love of my death?
Life and death do they go together?
People! Tell me.
Why must I live in a world that makes me cry?
A world that depresses me.
A world that is full of love but yet hates.
Why must I live?

Strength

Be strong, survive.
Although it hurts and you feel as if you can't go on,
It gets easier.
The pain you feel today will only be a memory
    tomorrow.
The scars we get from this life we live
Make us strong for the life we have yet to live.
The love I hold is for one and only one
I must keep that love till he wants me to
Place it in his hands.
I understand the feelings
He is feeling but yet knowing that
I can't force my love upon him
I fear only one thing,
That I may not ever be able
To give him this love.
Things change and so do people.
But yet this love will never be given to another

This poem was written for Tim. He never was in love
with me and the friendship would die as well. He
was a user of people just like Peter. It's hard to tell the
difference between those who will use us and those
who will be our balcony people.

To Be Happy

Things will be much brighter for
Everyone by the end of June or July.
The sun will shine and
Everyone will be happy
Like it should be.
Everyone should be happy
Everyone has to make him or herself happy.
Just remember to give
Of yourself is not that bad.
At least you know
You made someone else happy
Somewhere in the course of your life.
They will have worm memories of those times

Rejection

Rejection is something I never could handle
Afraid of it, I ran from it.
Tonight I faced it
Flat out, I asked if you love me.
You have began to see another
She is beautiful but the question
Was still there. I asked and shook in
My skin. The answer
Was a relief.
I know I will never lose you
Altogether but the possibility of
Never having you completely
I can only blame myself
Your happiness is what is important not mine
We all need to make others happy

Warm Memories

Looking at the clouds together.
Enjoying the beauty as two lovers
Enjoy the beauty of being together.
Even though the clouds are artificial
The love is not. Few moments spent
Together collected in the minds
Of two such lovers as
'Warm memories'
Hear the cries of lonely hearts
Bring them together as one
Forget the pain
And remember the warm memories
Make new ones
The heart doesn't forget the warmth
It believes in the happiness
Once shared by these two Lovers
Forget not the pain, but use it to grow
Never forget the memories that were so dear and are
So warm within your heart
Help others to grow and to believe
That warmth is there to be found.

Be Thankful

Be thankful for the time we
Have now for we no not the future
The past is gone and we must not
Hang on to it
What we make of out lives
Now is what we will make of them later
Love will be the key to all
The locked doors we may wonder upon

April

April 4th, 1990
As water crashes over the rocks
It reaches out to the beach
It grabs the white sand and pulls
It under to the ocean floor,
Never to be seen again
April 5, 1990
103 days filled with love and passion.
Is it all gone in one breath? Or is this a pause
In the flow of happiness?
Answers needed, but not heard

The Love

The love I hold is for one and only one
I must keep that love till he wants me to
Place it into his hands. I understand
The feelings he is feeling, but yet
Knowing that I can't force my love upon him.
I fear only one thing that I may not ever be
Able to give him that love.
Things change and so do people
But yet this love will never be given to another

Warm Memories II

The candle light flutters
Out silhouettes on the wall
An unforgettable night
A gift of love from god
We will try not to take it for granted
We pray that the newness will never end
Happiness, a state of mind, my mind with you
My heart with you
Days spent with innocents, my mind finds it
Hard to focus on anything but you
We treasure each moment spent as one
And moments apart we spend in warm memories
We spent the moments as if they were our last
But yet as if they would never end
What god holds for us in the future can only be love
And laughter. I thank him for bringing such
A beautiful person into my children's and my life
To David with love

I Can't

You say I'm drowning and I need to start to swim
Or learn how to swim
Even though I want to
I'm afraid to move
So don't cry when you hear that I've
Given up and drown
Remember the warm memories

Why

As I look to the sky
I wonder why
Things changed and so did I
Happy I may be but cry as I may
The love I hold is nothing but bold
But I shall care and love forever until I die

Baker

He smiles at me and I feel he likes me
Yet when it comes to flirting or
Going out with me he turns cold
How are you supposed to love?
Someone when someone is
Standing in his way?
Only if she would stop hurting him
Stop trying to keep him
He can't stand much more and when he hurts
I hurt
So therefore the revenge I have is not on him but her

Hidden Feelings

I try to hide my feelings
But it doesn't work.
You can see it in my eyes and feel it on my skin
I don't really understand the feelings I have
I can't tell you why I have them
You talk to me, it seems different
Totally confused I seem to find
Myself wondering about the times we have shared
Then I think about the future
When she may hurt you again
I can't bear to stand around and watch
For seeing you hurt the way you hurt me is
Something I'd rather not think of

To Mike With Thanks

We stand in a crowded room.
We all looking at the same exhibit
Do we see the same thing?
Most of us look at the obvious,
Some look further.
Those few, what do they see?
What are they tiny elves?
Looking for?
Maybe meaning, maybe life, maybe death.
But wait maybe elves.
Hidden among the obvious

The following poem I wrote when I was in a museum.
It shows that even then the spiral had begun to mold me.

The Ugliness of Beauty

Have you ever experienced never having anything
   because you have everything?
Well, I have.
People think that because I have fair looks and a fair
   body that I'm the one that always gets taken out on
   dates.
Well, I have some news for some of you, I don't.
Guys seem to think the same.
They think that I'm conceited and think I'm too good
   for them.
But one thing puzzles me; they never take the time to
   find out what I'm really like.
My friends make jokes about this so-called beauty.
It's kind of funny, but if I could,
I would give them some of that so called beauty as
   they call it.
People don't really look close enough to really see
   who or what I really am.
What they don't realize is that I'm really not beautiful.
They don't see me when I'm working hard to make
   myself look like someone.
They don't see me without my makeup or my hair in
   curlers.
They don't let me have the chance to prove to them
   that I'm just like any other girl,

I have feelings, too.
I care about what they have to say about me and the
  way I look to them.
With this experience I have had, I want you to
  remember one thing,
And that is before you start to gripe about the way
  someone looks,
Be they beautiful or not so pretty,
Remember they have feelings too.

As you can see in the beginning of the poem, I was
unable to even say that I was beautiful, afraid that
someone might read it and interpret it as conceit. You
can also see that at this point I was in the spiral that no
one wanted to be around me. Jokes from friends that I
thought that I was beautiful were hurting my feelings.
Anger had gotten to me and I would come out of this
with the feeling that I was worthless. I began to drink
again and, ultimately, another bad relationship and bad
ending would develop.

ABOUT THE AUTHOR

*M*ANY PEOPLE HAVE TRAUMAS in their lives as I have. However, most never get the real help they need. I have written this book in hopes that it will touch at least one person, to save one person from doing the unthinkable. I was born and raised in Colorado with its majestic peaks and beautiful weather. My parents raised six children (although I don't know how they did it). I am the youngest of two boys and four girls.

References

*H*ere are counseling clinics that help. I beg you, if you have gone through suffering, call one. Remember that it's not your fault. You didn't do anything to deserve the torture.

RAPE
Colorado Domestic Violence Coalition
Tel 303-573-9018
Rape Assistance and Awareness Program, P O Box 18951, Denver, CO 80218
303-322-RAPE (7273

PREGNANCY:
Birthright, Inc., Denver, 1631 Emerson St, Denver, CO 80218
Tel 303-832-2858/ 303-760-9077 (Emergency)
Planned Parenthood of The Rocky Mountain Teen Clinic (at all metro locations)
Tel 800-230-PLAN (7526)
Facts of Life Line
Tel 303-832-5995

ABUSE:
Family Tree Domestic Violence Shelter/ Women in Crisis Help Line
Tel 303-420-6752
Gateway Battered Women's Shelter
Tel 303-343-1851
Safe House Denver, Inc.
Tel 303-892-8900 (24 Hour Crisis Line)
Triad Shelter for Girls/Volunteers of America
Tel 303-831-8502 (24 Hours a Day, 7 Days a Week)
Violence Prevention Institute/Women's Crisis Center
Tel 303-688-84845 (24-Hour Crisis Line)

ALCOHOL & DRUGS:
Al-Anon/Alateen Service Center, 2801 E Colfax Ave St 204, Denver, CO 80206
Tel 303-321-8788
Arapahoe House, Inc
Tel 303-657-3700 (24 Hours a Day, 7 Days Week)
Mile High Council on Alcoholism and Drug Abuse, 1444 Wazee St, Denver, CO 80202
Tel 303-825-8113/ 800-850-9111

These numbers are taken from my local phone book. The people at the agencies are very understanding and can help you. Pick up the phone and talk to someone.